Classic Raclette Recipe

Chapter 1: Classic Raclette Recipe

Introduction to Raclette

Raclette is a traditional Swiss dish that originated in the Alpine regions. It is a delightful and indulgent meal that brings people together to enjoy the rich flavors of melted cheese, accompanied by a variety of accompaniments. The word "raclette" comes from the French word "racler," which means "to scrape," referring to the method of scraping the melted cheese onto different ingredients. In this chapter, we will explore the classic raclette recipe, from the ingredients and equipment needed to the step-by-step instructions for preparing this delicious dish.

Traditional Ingredients and Equipment

To make the classic raclette dish, you will need a few key ingredients and specialized equipment. Here are the traditional ingredients used in a raclette recipe:

1. Raclette Cheese: Raclette cheese is the star of the dish. It is a semi-hard cheese that melts beautifully, with a rich and nutty flavor. Look for authentic raclette cheese from Switzerland or opt for similar varieties from your local cheesemonger.

2. Potatoes: Potatoes are a staple in raclette meals. Choose waxy potatoes like Yukon Gold or Charlotte, as they hold their shape well when boiled or roasted.

3. Pickles: Pickles, such as cornichons or gherkins, add a tangy and crunchy element to the dish. Their acidic bite helps cut through the richness of the cheese.

4. Cured Meats: Cured meats like prosciutto, salami, or smoked ham are often served alongside raclette. Their savory and salty flavors complement the cheese beautifully.

5. Vegetables: Include a selection of vegetables like roasted bell peppers, grilled asparagus, or steamed broccoli to add freshness and balance to the meal.

6. Bread: Crusty bread, such as baguettes or country loaves, is a must-have for raclette. It serves as a vehicle for scooping up the melted cheese and adds texture to each bite.

As for equipment, you will need a raclette grill or a special raclette machine. These devices have individual trays or pans for melting the cheese and a heating element to keep the cheese warm and gooey. Some raclette grills also come with a cooking surface for grilling meats and vegetables.

Step-by-Step Instructions for Preparing the Classic Raclette Dish

Now let's dive into the step-by-step process of preparing the classic raclette dish:

1. Prepare the Potatoes: Start by washing and scrubbing the potatoes thoroughly. Peel them if desired or leave the skin on for added texture. Cut the potatoes into bite-sized pieces and cook them until tender. You can boil them in salted water or roast them in the oven with a drizzle of olive oil until golden brown.

2. Slice the Raclette Cheese: While the potatoes are cooking, slice the raclette cheese into thin, even slices. The slices should be thin enough to melt easily.

3. Prepare the Accompaniments: Arrange the pickles, cured meats, vegetables, and bread on a platter. This allows guests to help themselves and create their own personalized raclette combinations.

4. Heat the Raclette Grill: Preheat the raclette grill according to the manufacturer's instructions. Ensure that the heating element is hot enough to melt the cheese.

5. Melt the Cheese: Once the grill is hot, place a slice of raclette cheese in each individual tray or pan. Position the trays under the heating element and allow the cheese to melt slowly. As it starts to melt, use a scraper or a spatula to scrape the gooey cheese onto the accompaniments.

6. Serve and Enjoy: Once the cheese has melted and the accompaniments are ready, it's time

 to gather around the table and enjoy the raclette feast. Encourage guests to experiment with different combinations of cheese, potatoes, pickles, meats, and vegetables.

Serving Suggestions and Pairings

When serving the classic raclette dish, there are several ways to enhance the experience and create a memorable meal. Here are some serving suggestions and pairings:

1. Wine Pairings: Raclette pairs well with white wines such as Chasselas or Riesling. The crisp acidity and fruity flavors of these wines complement the richness of the cheese.

2. Additional Condiments: Offer condiments like mustard, chutneys, or honey to add another layer of flavor to the raclette. These condiments can be spread on bread or drizzled over the melted cheese.

3. Side Salads: Serve a simple side salad with fresh greens, cherry tomatoes, and a light vinaigrette to add a refreshing element to the meal.

4. Dessert: Finish off the raclette experience with a light and fruity dessert like a berry tart or a citrus sorbet. These desserts cleanse the palate and provide a satisfying end to the meal.

Tips and Variations for Personalizing Your Raclette Experience

To personalize your raclette experience, consider the following tips and variations:

1. Cheese Varieties: While raclette cheese is traditional, feel free to experiment with different types of melting cheese. Gruyère, Emmental, or Fontina are excellent alternatives that offer distinct flavors.

2. Seafood: Incorporate seafood into your raclette by adding cooked shrimp, smoked salmon, or scallops. The delicate flavors of seafood pair beautifully with the melted cheese.

3. Vegetarian Options: If you have vegetarian guests, offer a variety of grilled vegetables, marinated tofu, or vegetarian sausages as meat alternatives. This ensures everyone can enjoy the raclette experience.

4. Seasonal Ingredients: Take advantage of seasonal produce to add freshness and variety to your raclette. In summer, include grilled zucchini and fresh herbs, while in winter, roasted root vegetables and winter greens make excellent additions.

5. Experiment with Flavors: Explore different flavor combinations by incorporating spices, herbs, or infused oils into your raclette. Sprinkle smoked paprika, rosemary, or truffle oil over the melted cheese for a unique twist.

Remember, the beauty of raclette lies in its versatility and communal nature. Encourage your guests to get creative, try new combinations, and savor each cheesy bite. Enjoy the conviviality and warmth that raclette brings to the table.

Chapter 2: Creative Raclette Combinations

Exploring New Flavors and Ingredients for Raclette

Raclette is a versatile dish that offers endless possibilities for exploration and experimentation. In this chapter, we will delve into the world of creative raclette combinations, introducing new flavors and ingredients to elevate your raclette experience. Get ready to embark on a culinary adventure that will excite your taste buds and impress your guests.

Unique Pairings with Meats, Vegetables, and Fruits

When it comes to pairing raclette with meats, vegetables, and fruits, the options are vast. Here are some unique combinations to consider:

1. Meats:
- Spicy Chorizo: The smoky and spicy flavors of chorizo create a delightful contrast against the creamy raclette cheese. Slice the chorizo thinly and place it on a slice of bread before topping it with melted raclette.
- Bresaola and Arugula: The saltiness of bresaola, air-dried beef, pairs beautifully with the peppery arugula. Place a few slices of bresaola on a plate, top with a mound of arugula, and generously drizzle with melted raclette cheese.

2. Vegetables:
- Roasted Brussels Sprouts: Roast Brussels sprouts with olive oil, salt, and pepper until they are caramelized and tender. Serve them as a side dish alongside the raclette, allowing guests to dip the sprouts in the melted cheese.
- Grilled Eggplant: Slice eggplant into thick rounds, brush with olive oil, and grill until tender and charred. Arrange the grilled eggplant slices on a platter and drizzle with raclette cheese.

3. Fruits:

- Grilled Pineapple: Grilling pineapple brings out its natural sweetness and adds a smoky flavor. Cut pineapple into rings and grill until lightly charred. Serve the grilled pineapple with a generous dollop of raclette cheese for a sweet and savory combination.

- Caramelized Apples: Sauté apple slices in butter and brown sugar until they caramelize and become tender. Place the caramelized apples on a plate and generously pour melted raclette cheese over them. The sweet and tangy apples pair wonderfully with the rich and creamy cheese.

Step-by-Step Instructions for Innovative Raclette Creations

Now, let's explore some innovative raclette creations that go beyond the traditional melted cheese and accompaniments. These step-by-step instructions will guide you in preparing these delightful dishes:

1. Raclette Sliders:
- Step 1: Prepare small burger patties using your favorite ground meat, seasoned with salt, pepper, and your preferred spices.
- Step 2: Grill or pan-fry the burger patties until they reach your desired level of doneness.
- Step 3: Cut slider buns in half and lightly toast them.
- Step 4: Place a slice of raclette cheese on each burger patty and broil or use a culinary torch to melt the cheese.
- Step 5: Assemble the sliders by placing the cheesy patties on the bottom half of the buns, and add your desired toppings such as lettuce, tomato, pickles, and condiments.
- Step 6: Place the top bun on each slider and serve them warm, allowing the melted raclette to ooze out with each bite.

2. Raclette Tacos:
- Step 1: Prepare your favorite taco fillings, such as seasoned ground beef, grilled chicken, or sautéed vegetables.
- Step 2: Warm soft taco shells in a dry skillet or on a griddle.
- Step 3: Fill each taco shell with your chosen fillings.
- Step 4: Top the fillings with a generous amount of melted raclette cheese.
- Step 5: Add fresh toppings like diced tomatoes, shredded lettuce, sliced avocado, and a drizzle of salsa or hot sauce.
- Step 6: Serve the raclette tacos hot, allowing the cheese to melt further and bind all the flavors together.

3. Raclette Pizza:
- Step 1: Preheat your oven to the highest temperature possible.
- Step 2: Roll out pizza dough to your desired thickness and shape.
- Step 3: Spread your favorite pizza sauce on the dough, leaving a border for the crust.
- Step 4: Sprinkle grated raclette cheese evenly over the sauce.
- Step 5: Add your preferred toppings, such as cooked bacon, sautéed mushrooms, sliced bell peppers, and onions.
- Step 6: Place the pizza on a baking sheet or pizza stone and bake in the preheated oven until the cheese is bubbly and the crust is golden brown.
- Step 7: Remove from the oven, let it cool for a few minutes, slice, and serve.

Presenting Raclette in Different Forms (e.g., sliders, tacos, pizza)

Raclette doesn't have to be limited to the traditional presentation. By incorporating raclette into different forms, you can add variety and excitement to your raclette dining experience. Here are a few creative ways to present raclette:

1. Raclette Fondue:
- Set up a raclette machine with individual pans filled with melted raclette cheese.
- Provide skewers or fondue forks for guests to dip their desired ingredients into the melted cheese.
- Offer a selection of bite-sized vegetables, bread cubes, and cooked meats for dipping.

2. Raclette Stuffed Potatoes:
- Bake or boil large potatoes until tender.
- Slice off the top of each potato and scoop out the flesh, leaving a shell.

- Mix the potato flesh with melted raclette cheese, cooked bacon, and herbs of your choice.
- Fill the potato shells with the raclette mixture and bake until the cheese is melted and bubbly.
- Serve the raclette-stuffed potatoes as a hearty and flavorful side dish.

3. Raclette Skewers:
- Cut raclette cheese into cubes.
- Thread the cheese cubes onto skewers, alternating with your choice of grilled vegetables and cooked meats.
- Grill the skewers until the cheese is melted and the ingredients are heated through.
- Serve the raclette skewers as a fun and interactive appetizer or main course.

Serving Suggestions for a Memorable Dining Experience

To create a memorable dining experience with your creative raclette combinations, consider the following serving suggestions:

1. Aesthetically Pleasing Platters: Arrange your meats, vegetables, fruits, and other accompaniments on platters or boards, creating a visually appealing spread. Use a variety of colors and textures to make the presentation enticing.

2. Interactive Stations: Set up interactive stations where guests can assemble their own raclette creations. Provide different options and encourage guests to get creative with their combinations.

3. Garnishes and Sauces: Offer a variety of garnishes and sauces to enhance the flavors. Fresh herbs, spices, flavored oils, and specialty sauces can elevate the taste profile of each raclette combination.

4. Seasonal Ingredients: Incorporate seasonal ingredients into your raclette combinations to highlight their freshness and flavor. Consider using locally sourced produce and ingredients to support local farmers and producers.

5. Wine and Beverage Pairings: Pair your creative raclette combinations with suitable wines or other beverages. Consult with a sommelier or explore different flavor profiles to find the perfect match for each dish.

Remember, the key to a memorable raclette dining experience lies in the combination of flavors, textures, and presentation. Be adventurous, think outside the box, and have fun creating your unique raclette creations.

Chapter 3: Raclette Desserts and Sweets

Unconventional Raclette Creations for Sweet Tooths

Raclette is often associated with savory dishes, but it can also be used to create indulgent and delightful desserts. In this chapter, we will explore the world of raclette desserts and sweets, introducing unconventional creations that will satisfy any sweet tooth. Get ready to indulge in the creamy and versatile nature of raclette cheese, as we dive into the realm of delectable desserts.

Using Raclette Cheese in Desserts and Snacks

Raclette cheese, with its creamy texture and subtle nutty flavor, can add a unique twist to desserts and snacks.

Here are some ideas on how to incorporate raclette cheese into sweet creations:

1. Raclette Cheesecake:
- Replace traditional cream cheese with raclette cheese in your favorite cheesecake recipe. The melted raclette cheese adds a smooth and creamy texture, along with a hint of savory depth to the dessert. Pair it with a graham cracker crust or a chocolate cookie base for a delicious twist on the classic cheesecake.

2. Raclette Filled Pastries:
- Stuff puff pastry or filo dough with melted raclette cheese and your choice of sweet fillings like caramelized apples, berries, or chocolate. Bake until the pastries are golden brown and the cheese is gooey and melted. The combination of the flaky pastry and the creamy raclette filling creates a delightful treat.

3. Raclette Chocolate Fondue:
- Prepare a chocolate fondue and add melted raclette cheese to the mix. The addition of raclette cheese adds a creamy and savory note to the sweet chocolate, creating a unique and decadent dipping experience. Serve the fondue with an array of fruits, marshmallows, and other dippable treats.

Step-by-Step Instructions for Preparing Raclette-Based Sweets

To help you create raclette-based sweets, here are step-by-step instructions for a couple of delicious desserts:

1. Raclette Cheesecake Bars:
- Step 1: Preheat your oven and prepare a baking dish lined with parchment paper.
- Step 2: In a mixing bowl, combine crushed graham crackers or cookies with melted butter and press the mixture evenly into the bottom of the prepared baking dish.

- Step 3: In a separate bowl, beat together raclette cheese, sugar, eggs, vanilla extract, and any additional flavorings you desire until smooth and creamy.
- Step 4: Pour the raclette cheese mixture over the crust in the baking dish.
- Step 5: Bake in the preheated oven until the edges are set and the center is slightly jiggly.
- Step 6: Allow the cheesecake bars to cool completely before refrigerating for a few hours or overnight.
- Step 7: Cut the chilled cheesecake into bars and serve chilled or at room temperature.

2. Raclette and Caramelized Apple Tart:
- Step 1: Preheat your oven and prepare a tart shell or use a pre-made one.
- Step 2: In a skillet, melt butter and add sliced apples. Cook over medium heat until the apples caramelize and become tender.
- Step 3: Spread a layer of raclette cheese over the tart shell.

- Step 4: Arrange the caramelized apples on top of the cheese.
- Step 5: Optional: Sprinkle a mixture of cinnamon and sugar over the apples for extra flavor.
- Step 6: Bake the tart in the preheated oven until the crust is golden brown and the cheese is melted and bubbly.
- Step 7: Remove from the oven and let it cool slightly before slicing and serving.

Pairing Raclette with Fruits, Chocolates, and Other Dessert Ingredients

To create harmonious flavors in your raclette desserts, it's essential to pair raclette cheese with complementary ingredients. Here are some suggestions for pairing raclette with fruits, chocolates, and other dessert ingredients:

1. Fruits:
- Berries: The tartness of berries like raspberries, strawberries, or blueberries pairs beautifully with the creamy raclette cheese. Serve a bowl of fresh berries alongside raclette-based desserts or incorporate them directly into the dessert itself.
- Caramelized Apples: The combination of caramelized apples and raclette cheese creates a balance of sweet and savory flavors. Use caramelized apples as a topping or filling for raclette desserts to add a touch of natural sweetness.

2. Chocolates:
- Dark Chocolate: The richness and bitterness of dark chocolate can be complemented by the creamy and slightly savory raclette cheese. Dip pieces of raclette cheese in melted dark chocolate for a unique sweet-savory treat.

- Milk Chocolate: The creamy and smooth texture of milk chocolate pairs well with the milder flavor of raclette cheese. Use melted milk chocolate as a drizzle or topping over raclette-based desserts for an added touch of indulgence.

3. Other Dessert Ingredients:
- Nuts: Incorporate toasted and chopped nuts, such as almonds, walnuts, or hazelnuts, into raclette desserts for added crunch and nutty flavors. Sprinkle them over the desserts or mix them into fillings or crusts.
- Honey or Maple Syrup: Drizzle honey or maple syrup over raclette desserts to enhance their sweetness and add a natural sweetness that complements the cheese's flavors.

Tips for Balancing Savory and Sweet Flavors in Raclette Desserts

Balancing savory and sweet flavors in raclette desserts can be a delicate task. Here are some tips to help you achieve a harmonious blend of flavors:

1. Moderation: Use raclette cheese in moderation to avoid overpowering the sweetness of the desserts. The cheese should enhance the flavors without dominating them.

2. Choose Complementary Ingredients: Select ingredients that naturally pair well with both raclette cheese and the other sweet components of your dessert. Look for ingredients that add depth, richness, or contrasting flavors to create a balanced taste profile.

3. Experiment with Flavors: Don't be afraid to experiment with different flavors and ingredients to find your perfect balance. Test small batches or variations of your desserts to refine the recipe and adjust the seasoning or cheese quantity as needed.

4. Presentation: Pay attention to the presentation of your raclette desserts. Aesthetically pleasing plating can enhance the overall dining experience and make the desserts more enticing.

Remember, raclette desserts provide an opportunity to explore the unique versatility of raclette cheese and surprise your guests with unexpected flavors. Embrace your creativity and enjoy the process of crafting delectable raclette-based sweets.

Conclusion:

In conclusion, raclette is not only limited to its traditional form of melted cheese and accompaniments but also offers endless possibilities for creativity and innovation. By exploring new flavors, ingredients, and presentation styles, you can elevate your raclette experience and create memorable dining moments for yourself and your guests.

In this book, we have covered a range of raclette recipes, from the classic dish to creative combinations and even sweet desserts. We have provided step-by-step instructions, pairing suggestions, and tips for personalizing your raclette experience. Whether you're a seasoned chef or a novice cook, these recipes are designed to inspire you and encourage you to experiment with flavors and techniques.

As you embark on your raclette journey, here is a final list of tips to keep in mind:

1. Quality Ingredients: Use high-quality raclette cheese, along with fresh and seasonal ingredients, to enhance the flavors of your dishes.

2. Equipment: Invest in a good raclette grill or machine that allows for easy melting of the cheese and provides a fun and interactive dining experience.

3. Pairing and Presentation: Experiment with different pairings, be it meats, vegetables, fruits, or desserts, to create interesting flavor combinations. Pay attention to the presentation of your dishes to make them visually appealing and enticing.

4. Personalization: Feel free to personalize your raclette experience by adding your favorite spices, herbs, or condiments to the dishes. Don't be afraid to think outside the box and get creative with your combinations.

5. Balance Savory and Sweet: When incorporating raclette into desserts, maintain a balance between the savory nature of the cheese and the sweetness of the other ingredients. Test small batches and adjust seasoning as needed.

6. Seasonal Variations: Embrace seasonal produce and ingredients to add freshness and depth to your raclette dishes.

7. Exploration and Fun: The beauty of raclette lies in its versatility and the opportunity it presents to explore new flavors and techniques. Enjoy the process, be open to experimentation, and have fun creating your own raclette masterpieces.

With these tips and the recipes provided in this book, you are well-equipped to embark on a flavorful and exciting journey through the world of raclette. Whether you're hosting a dinner party, planning a cozy family gathering, or simply treating yourself to a delicious meal, raclette is sure to impress and delight.

So, gather your loved ones, fire up the raclette grill, and let the aromas and flavors of raclette transport you to a world of culinary delight. Happy cooking and bon appétit!

Manufactured by Amazon.ca
Bolton, ON